THE HOW AND WHY WONDER® BOOK OF
ELECTRICITY

By Jerome J. Notkin, Ed. D., Science Supervisor, Suffolk County, N.Y.
and Sidney Gulkin, M.S. in Ed., Teacher, New York City

Illustrated by Robert Patterson and Charles Bernard

Edited under the supervision of
  Dr. Paul E. Blackwood,
  Washington, D. C.

Text and illustrations approved by
  Oakes A. White, Brooklyn Children's Museum, Brooklyn, New York

PRICE/STERN/SLOAN
Publishers, Inc., Los Angeles
1983

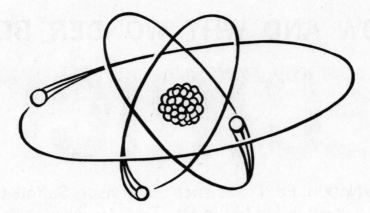

INTRODUCTION

When a town stands still for eight hours, it is missing something mighty important. One such town stood still because the electricity stopped. This was most inconvenient for everyone, but it did make a boy named Mike and his sister Susan Jane think about it. They were filled with questions: What is electricity? How do we make electricity? How does electricity get to our town?

Just as Mike and his sister explore the wonders of electricity with their father, so will inquisitive children everywhere get answers to their questions about electricity as they read this book. Like the others in the *How and Why Wonder®Book* series, this science book is authentic and colorful and can be read with interest by the whole family.

The answers to questions about electricity that are now easy to give young people are the answers which stretched the minds of the greatest scientists less than a hundred years ago. Fortunately, books give children the wealth of information which took so long for scientists to discover.

Thinking, investigating and experimenting are the special paths which are basic to science. This book, which includes more than a dozen experiments to help readers discover what others have found before, will lead children along these same paths. It is an excellent addition to the school or home collection of science books for young readers and their parents.

Paul E. Blackwood

Dr. Blackwood is a professional employee in the U. S. Office of Education. This book was edited by him in his private capacity and no official support or endorsement by the Office of Education is intended or should be inferred.

Copyright© 1960, 1969, 1975 by Price/Stern/Sloan Publishers, Inc.
Published by Price/Stern/Sloan Publishers, Inc.
410 North La Cienega Boulevard, Los Angeles, California 90048

ISBN: 0-8431-4259-6

Library of Congress Catalog Card Number 61-1578

How and Why Wonder® Books is a trademark of Price/Stern/Sloan Publishers, Inc.

CONTENTS

THE DAY THE TOWN STOOD STILL

Why is the main electrical cable the lifeline of a modern industrial town?

THIS story is not made up. It is true. It really happened. My town stood still for eight hours. Why? We had no electricity.

My house was not the same. The bells didn't ring. My mother's washing machine stopped dead. Our television set was dark and silent. The little radio in my room was just a box without a voice. Our electric stove joined the washing machine, radio, and refrigerator. The electric clock in the kitchen was stopped at 10:36 A.M. That's when it happened. Mother changed the fuses. That was no help.

Our neighbor came running to us for help. Nothing was working in her house, either. She was really worried. Her baby's formula needed refrigeration. The food was becoming spoiled. She tried to call the doctor for her sick baby. But her phone was not working either.

My mother drove her in the car to pick up the doctor. When she arrived at the gas station to fill up the tank she was told that the pumps were not working. Several cars were stuck in the middle of the road. No gas!

Then mother turned the car radio on. It worked! It worked on the storage battery. The radio was full of news.

"Main cable at the power station destroyed by explosion. . . . Repairs are under way, but it will take at least eight hours. . . . Motorists are urged to give help to those who need it most."

So that was it! The main electrical cable had been damaged.

"Why is that cable so important?" I asked my mother.

"That cable is like the main pipe supplying us with water, Mike," my mother replied. "When that pipe is broken, the water stops running. There is just no other way of getting water. And there is no other way of getting electrical power until that cable is repaired."

How are we dependent upon electricity? By the time Dad came home it was dark. We helped him get into the house by flashlight. We had two candles — one in the kitchen, another in the living room.

We had our cold dinner by candle-light. My sister, Susan Jane, and I had a lot of fun, but Mother and Dad didn't think it was so funny.

The people on my street walked about with flashlights, knocking on each others' doors instead of ringing door-bells.

Everyone was excited.

"When will the lights go on?" people asked.

"Soon, soon," my Dad replied.

It seemed that a long time passed before the lights suddenly came on. The buzz of the refrigerator started. My little radio was on at full volume. The television set suddenly came to life with picture and sound.

It seemed as if the sun had suddenly begun to shine in the middle of the night.

My town began to move again!

WHAT IS THIS MAGICAL THING CALLED ELECTRICITY?

In what ways does a waterfall serve us?

"ELECTRICITY, or electrical power, just doesn't happen," said Dad. "It has to be made. How? What things are used to make it? Let's see.

"When my grandfather ground his wheat," said Dad, "he had to take it to a mill that was near a waterfall."

"Why near a waterfall?" I asked.

"Well, Mike," said Dad, "they used the waterfall for the power to run the mill. If you have never seen one, or don't know how it works, we can build a model. We need a cheese box, a stick for an axle or shaft, and some jar covers for blades.

"When water falls on these covers or blades, the shaft goes around, and it, in turn, moves wheels and gears. You see, then, that the fuel used to turn these wheels is free. The water moves the blades and the mill is in business."

"That's terrific, Dad, but how does falling water make electricity?" I asked.

THIS IS A HYDROELECTRIC DAM RUN BY WATER POWER, OR THE FORCE CAUSED BY THE DIFFERENCE IN ELEVATION OF THE WATER BEHIND AND BELOW THE DAM. WATER POWER MAY BE DESCRIBED AS THE POWER OF WATER USED TO MOVE OR DRIVE A MACHINE. THE FLOW OF WATER IN RIVERS AND STREAMS IS A SOURCE OF ENERGY. WHEN THE WATER, WHICH HAS BEEN COLLECTING BEHIND THE DAM, RUSHES DOWN, THIS ENERGY TURNS THE GENERATOR AND PRODUCES ELECTRICITY.

What are some of the ways we know of to make electricity?

"To make electricity which will not only turn a mill, but send out the electrons through roads made of wire, shafts have to be turned inside a tunnel, called a generator or dynamo. Water very often supplies the power to turn the shafts that make or generate this magical electricity."

"Oh, yes. We learned about some of these places in school. There is Hoover Dam, Niagara Falls, the dams of the Tennessee Valley Authority, Grand Coulee and Bonneville dams, and many others like them."

"Very good, Mike," smiled Dad. "And power from these places is sent hundreds of miles to homes, factories, farms and schools. It even runs railroads and subways."

"Really, Dad? Can water power do all that? But suppose there are no waterfalls or dams nearby?"

THERE ARE DIFFERENT KINDS OF POWER PLANTS, BUT THEY ALL HAVE SOMETHING IN COMMON. EACH POWER PLANT HAS A GENERATOR WHERE ELECTRICITY IS MADE. THIS IS A COAL-BURNING POWER PLANT. WATER IS HEATED BY A COAL FIRE AND STEAM MAKES THE GENERATOR MOVE.

What kind of power is used to run subways?

"The scientists and engineers have thought about that. They have figured out ways to make electricity from other things. Take coal as an example. That can help make electricity for use anywhere. Do you know that subways in many of our large cities run on coal-made electricity?"

"That's real magic!" said my sister, who had been listening quietly all along.

"No, Susan Jane, I wouldn't say it is magic. I like to call it science. It can be explained and used by everyone, not only by magicians."

"Does it work like the dams?" Susan Jane asked.

"Something like it," Dad continued. "In the case of dams, water goes into a pipe where it turns the blades of the large wheels. Coal is often used to heat water and convert it into steam which goes into the pipes. The large wheels are called turbines."

GENERATOR

TURBINE

What makes the generator spin around?

"Is this turbine connected to anything?" I asked.

"Oh, yes. It's the turbine that makes the generator spin around. Electricity comes out the other side."

Susan Jane looked puzzled. She asked, "What is a generator? What does it do? How does it work?"

"I'll show you," said Dad. "We can make a model of a generator. But we'll need some things. Susan Jane, bring Mother's teakettle. Mike, bring your magnet and your flashlight. I have the other things we need."

What part does the steam play in this experiment? Susan Jane and I ran to get these things, wondering how the kettle was going to be used.

"Now, then," said Dad when we returned, "watch and you will see how a generator makes electricity. The fire heats the water in the kettle. That makes the steam, just as burning coal can boil water to make steam. It is this steam power that pushes against the blades of the turbine. My turbine is made of cardboard, but it gives you the idea. Then the turbine turns the magnet inside a coil of electrical wire."

"Is a magnet really used?" I asked.

In what way are electrons pushed? "Yes. It is a magnet made by electricity, called an electromagnet. There are many turns of covered wire wound around an iron core. As the magnet moves inside a coil of wire, it pushes tiny things called electrons. When electrons are pushed or moved, electricity flows. That is why the light bulb that I removed from your flashlight goes on."

"Gosh, Dad, just think — a magnet and a wire make our television sets work!" I said.

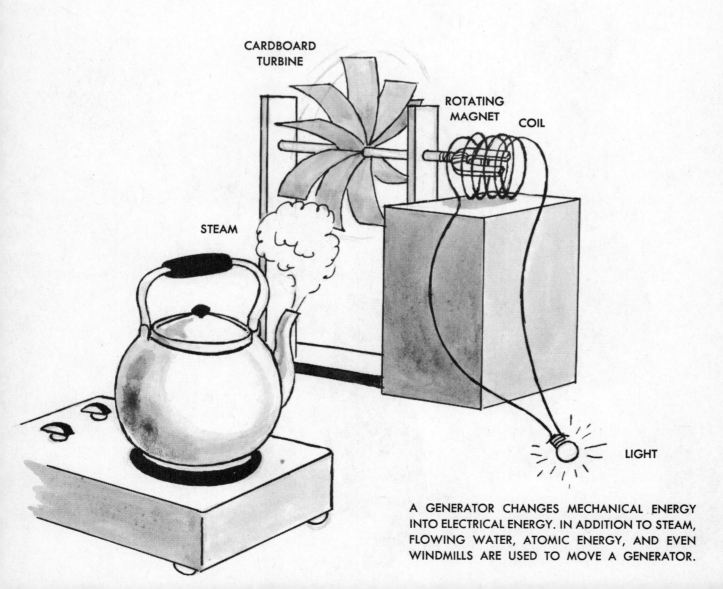

CARDBOARD TURBINE

ROTATING MAGNET

COIL

STEAM

LIGHT

A GENERATOR CHANGES MECHANICAL ENERGY INTO ELECTRICAL ENERGY. IN ADDITION TO STEAM, FLOWING WATER, ATOMIC ENERGY, AND EVEN WINDMILLS ARE USED TO MOVE A GENERATOR.

A BATTERY IN A FLASHLIGHT OR PORTABLE RADIO IS REALLY A KIND OF POWER STATION. SUCH BATTERIES ARE CALLED DRY CELLS. WE CALL THEM "DRY" BECAUSE THE WET ACID PASTE INSIDE A CELL IS SEALED UP TIGHT AND CANNOT SPILL OUT.

"Right, Mike. But remember, it is not this toy magnet and not this small piece of wire. It is a large electro-magnet turning inside a huge coil of wire. It looks more like a tunnel. The more wire in the coil, the more electrons can be moved. And we get more electricity.

Why is a cell called a portable power station?

"Do you mean that my flashlight and portable radio carry a generator inside of them just for me, every time I want to use it?" I asked, looking at my flashlight.

"That's right. The battery is its own power station."

YOUR PORTABLE POWER STATION

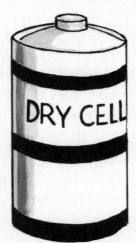

11

POWER STATION

TRANSFORMER

HIGHWAYS THAT CARRY ELECTRICITY

How does a transformer help us get electricity to our homes?

"HOW DO these electrons travel all the way from the power station to us?" I wanted to know.

"I was coming to that. Do you know that as we ride along the highways there are electrical highways right above our heads that we hardly ever notice? Sometimes they are even under the roads."

"What are they for?" Susan Jane asked.

"They are the highways of wire where those invisible electrons are flowing toward homes, factories and farms," Dad answered. "The electricity has to be delivered where it is needed and in the right amount. Instead of trucks and trains that carry off goods from factories, wire or cables do the job here. They do it quietly, without any fuss."

"How do the wires do it?" asked my sister.

"Well, all along the roads where the electricity is carried are devices called transformers. They change electric current from a high to a low voltage, or the reverse, and allow the wires to carry more electrical current."

SUB-STATION

TRANSFORMER

TRANSFORMERS

ELECTRICITY FROM THE POWER STATION IS CARRIED THROUGH WIRES TO HOMES, FAC-
TORIES, STORES, FARMS AND SCHOOLS. TRANSFORMERS HELP IN THE TRANSPORTATION
OF ELECTRICITY FROM THE POWER STATION TO ALL THESE PLACES. A TRANSFORMER IS
A MACHINE THAT TRANSFORMS OR CHANGES AN ELECTRIC CURRENT FROM A HIGH TO
A LOW VOLTAGE. IT CAN ALSO CHANGE CURRENT FROM A LOW TO A HIGH VOLTAGE.
THE TEXT AND ILLUSTRATIONS BEGINNING ON PAGE 19 WILL FURTHER EXPLAIN THE
FUNCTION OF A TRANSFORMER.

Why is copper most commonly used for electrical wiring? "The wires or cables are made of material that must be a good conductor or carrier. It's like having a good clear road without bumps and rocks for cars to travel over. Good conductors are usually made of copper."

"Is copper the only conductor of electricity?" I asked.

"No. There are other ones. Silver is the best, but it's too expensive to use. Aluminum is also a good conductor and is gaining wider use because of its lightness. We use millions of tons of copper to make electrical wire for all purposes."

Why don't we use copper wires in our toaster? "Do we always use copper?" Susan Jane wanted to know.

"No," said Dad. "Take our toaster, for example. The curled-up wires inside of it happen to be poor conductors."

"Wouldn't that mean that when electricity tries to get through, it will have a tough job?" I asked. I was puzzled.

Dad smiled. "What happens in a toaster? The wires get red hot. This shows us that electricity is having a difficult job passing through. But it makes our toast taste good. In an electric stove it broils our steaks and chops and cooks our meals. That's not all. Mother's electric iron uses these poor conductors or carriers, too. Otherwise the flat bottom of the iron would not get hot enough to iron our shirts, tablecloths and other things.

Can you name three electrical things in your home that use poor conductors? "There are many other uses for these poor conductors. Can you name some other appliances which might have them?"

"Heating pads."

"Coffee makers."

"Waffle irons."

"An electric heater."

"An electric frying pan."

"That's enough," laughed Dad. "Now let's ask Mother to put electricity to work and prepare some lunch. This talk about steak and chops is making me hungry."

"Me, too," we echoed, and everyone went into the kitchen.

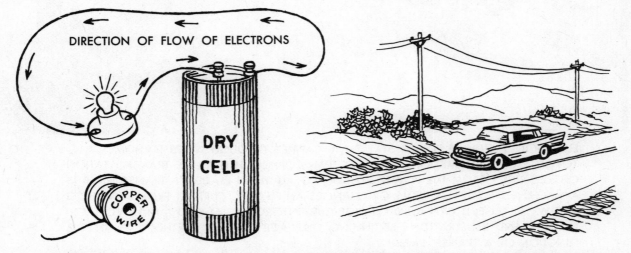

DIRECTION OF FLOW OF ELECTRONS

DRY CELL

COPPER WIRE

COPPER IS ONE OF THE BEST CONDUCTORS OF ELECTRIC CURRENT, AND IT IS USED WIDELY IN THE MANUFACTURE OF THIN ELECTRICAL WIRE, AS WELL AS THE HEAVIER CABLES ALONG HIGHWAYS.

ELECTRICITY IS REALLY A FIRST COUSIN OF MAGNETS

Are magnets and electricity related?

"YOU know, Dad, one of the things that you said yesterday still confuses me. What does the electrical magnet have to do with making electricity? I know that magnets have some kind of power. They can attract nails and other things. But how do magnets help us make electricity?"

While I was talking, Susan Jane was picking things up with my magnet.

"Magnets and electricity are in the same family," explained Dad. "We might even say they are cousins. We can try something to clear this up."

MAGNETS HAVE A DRAWING OR PULLING POWER, AND ATTRACT THINGS MADE OF STEEL, IRON AND NICKEL.

THE WORD *MAGNETISM* COMES FROM THE NAME *MAGNESIA*, AN ANCIENT CITY OF ASIA, WHERE MANY LOADSTONES WERE FOUND. THE LOADSTONE, ALSO SPELLED LODE-STONE, IS A MAGNETIC ROCK, AND WAS USED BY ANCIENT PEOPLES IN THE SAILING OF SHIPS. LIKE A COMPASS NEEDLE, A PIECE OF LOADSTONE ROCK WILL POINT NORTH.

"Can we help?" begged Susan Jane.

"Why, sure. Mike, bring down your scout compass. Susan Jane, bring the cover of your crayon box."

When we returned, Dad had removed the dry cell from my flashlight.

"Put the compass into the cover," Dad instructed. "Wind some insulated wire about eight or ten times around the cover."

What happens when electricity flows through a wire?

Then Dad touched one end of the wire, which had been stripped back, to the bottom of the dry cell, and he touched the other end to the center part at the top of the cell.

"Did you see what happened?" asked Dad.

"Yes, the needle of Mike's compass moved."

"That's right. You know that one magnet can move another magnet. When electricity went through the wire, the needle, which is a magnet, moved. That means that, somewhere, there was another magnet. When electricity flows through wires, there is magnetism around the wires."

"Can we see it?" asked Susan Jane.

"No. Not any more than we can see magnetism pulling nails to Mike's magnet. But the magnetism is there, all right."

"I'm not sure I understand," I said.

HANS CHRISTIAN OERSTED DISCOVERED THAT ELECTRICITY AND MAGNETISM WERE RELATED. IN THE YEAR 1820, OERSTED OBSERVED THAT WHEN HE SENT AN ELECTRIC CURRENT THROUGH A WIRE THAT WAS NEAR A COMPASS, THE COMPASS NEEDLE MOVED. HE SHOWED THAT THE FLOW OF ELECTRICITY THROUGH A WIRE CAUSES A MAGNETISM AROUND THE WIRE. MICHAEL FARADAY ALSO EXPERIMENTED WITH ELECTRICITY AND MAGNETISM. HIS IMPORTANT WORK RESULTED IN THE FIRST ELECTRIC GENERATOR.

What happens when a magnet moves inside a coil of wire?

"You will soon, Mike. If a magnet moves when electrons go through a coil of wire, would electrons move when a magnet passes through a coil? This puzzled a scientist several hundred years ago, and he decided to experiment. His experiment worked, and that marked the beginning of many wonderful things.

"If we use a small magnet and a small wire, only a few electrons would move. But when we move very powerful magnets inside thousands of coils, many electrons flow. It doesn't matter whether the magnets or the coils move, but it's the movement which generates the electricity."

"I understand it more clearly now, Dad."

"Good. As you see, there's nothing magical about it," said Dad. "But let's back up a bit. Do you remember that I kept tapping one end of the wire to the dry cell to make the compass move? We can do it easier if we use a switch, such as we have in our house."

"Does it make any difference if it's an up-and-down switch or one that we use to ring the doorbell?" asked Susan Jane.

How is a switch like a door?

"Not one bit," answered Dad. "Each one can turn something on and off. When we close any switch, the connection is completed and the electrons can flow again. When we open the switch, the connection is broken and the electrons cannot flow."

Susan Jane exclaimed, "That's just like opening or closing a gate or door."

"Of course! That's a nice way to put it," complimented Dad. "Did you ever hear the expression, 'completing the circuit' or 'breaking the circuit'? That's what is meant. When the switch is closed, the light, the refrigerator, the waffle iron, the coffee maker, and your electric train, all go on. When we turn the switch off, these appliances go off."

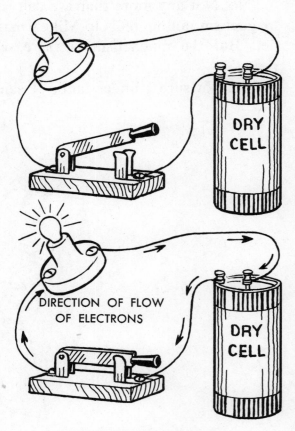

DIRECTION OF FLOW OF ELECTRONS

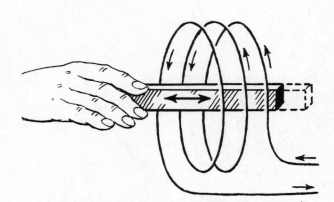

THE MOVEMENT OF A MAGNET INSIDE A COIL OF WIRE GENERATES ELECTRICITY.

TOP: BREAKING THE CIRCUIT.
BOTTOM: COMPLETING THE CIRCUIT.

IRON CORE

OUR HOMES ARE OFTEN SUPPLIED WITH 110 VOLTS OF ELECTRICITY, BUT TOY ELECTRIC TRAINS, FOR EXAMPLE, NEED FEWER VOLTS TO OPERATE. STEP-DOWN TRANSFORMERS STEP DOWN, OR DE-CREASE, THE VOLTAGE OF AN ALTERNATING CURRENT, ENABLING A TOY TRAIN TO RUN.

50 TURNS

5 TURNS

11 VOLTS A.C. TO RUN TOY TRAIN →

→ 110 VOLTS A.C.

ELECTRICITY NEEDS TRANSFORMERS

Why is your toy train transformer called a step-down transformer?

"DOESN'T the train set you gave me for my birthday work from my transformer? I never really knew what that word meant," I said.

"Let's look it up in the dictionary," suggested Susan Jane.

"A good idea," said Dad. "Let's see. Transform means, 'to change in form.'

"When we use a transformer for a train, we plug it into the wall socket. Our home is supplied with 110 volts of electricity. Our train uses much less, perhaps eight to twelve volts. How can we cut it down?"

"Does the transformer do the job for us?" I wanted to know.

"Yes, it does. It steps it down, just as it does in other parts of the house. We have a transformer to step down the voltage before it goes into our door-bell. We could use batteries, too, but we'd have to replace them when they were used up."

"How does a transformer work?" Susan Jane asked.

"Very simply, it works like this," said Dad. "There are two coils of wire, one larger than the other. If current is sent through the first coil, magnetism surrounds it. The second coil is affected by the magnetism and electricity comes out of its wires.

"If the second coil is larger than the first coil, higher voltage comes out than went into the original coil. If the second coil is smaller, as in your train set, less voltage comes out.

"The transformer raises or lowers the voltage of the current. We can step it up or step it down.

"Remember, when we speak of current, we mean A.C., or alternating current. Dry cells and storage batteries are all D.C., or direct current."

"Are these transformers used only in toy trains and in doorbells?" inquired Susan Jane.

"No. Their most important use is in changing the voltage of electricity from the power station, a steam-turbine, hydroelectric, or atomic power plant, to places many miles away.

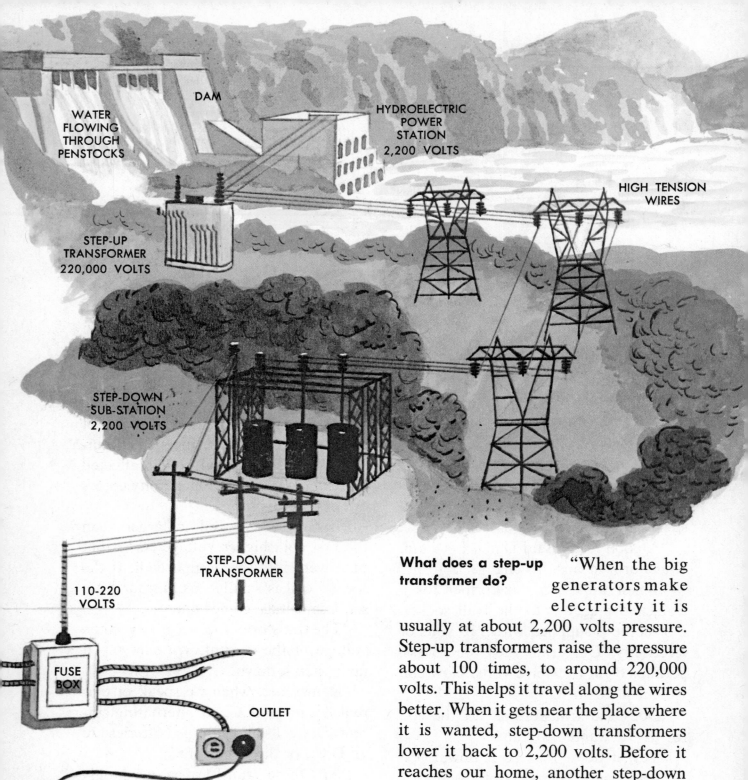

DAM

WATER
FLOWING
THROUGH
PENSTOCKS

HYDROELECTRIC
POWER
STATION
2,200 VOLTS

HIGH TENSION
WIRES

STEP-UP
TRANSFORMER
220,000 VOLTS

STEP-DOWN
SUB-STATION
2,200 VOLTS

STEP-DOWN
TRANSFORMER

110-220
VOLTS

FUSE
BOX

OUTLET

TRAIN
TRANSFORMER

8-12 VOLTS

What does a step-up transformer do?

"When the big generators make electricity it is usually at about 2,200 volts pressure. Step-up transformers raise the pressure about 100 times, to around 220,000 volts. This helps it travel along the wires better. When it gets near the place where it is wanted, step-down transformers lower it back to 2,200 volts. Before it reaches our home, another step-down transformer lowers it to 110 volts. In some homes, 220 volts are used.

"As you see, these wonderful machines increase pressure or voltage. They also act as shrinkers of voltage."

WE MUST OBSERVE SAFETY RULES

"DO YOU remember when I had my arm in a sling? That was a very bad burn I received as a result of carelessness with electricity," Dad told us.

"How did it happen?" Susan Jane wanted to know.

"I tried to plug in my electric razor while my hands were wet," Dad explained. "I am pretty lucky to be alive. I was so badly burned that the doctor had to treat me for several weeks before I could use my hand.

Can you remember at least five "never" rules?

"If you really want to have fun with electricity," said Dad, "you must first learn to play the important game of NEVER."

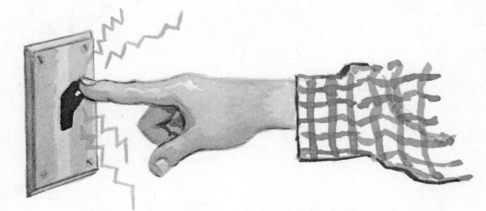

NEVER touch a switch with wet or damp hands. Water is a conductor. You might be badly burned or receive a severe shock. When you touch a switch, or any electric appliance, be sure your hands are dry.

NEVER overload your connections. Don't try to plug too many electric appliances into one home appliance circuit. It is dangerous and can cause a short circuit or fire.

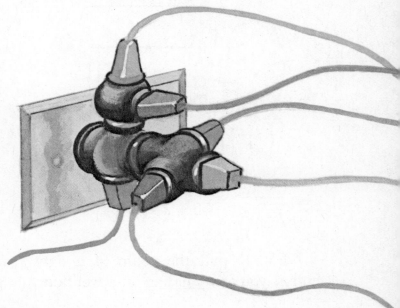

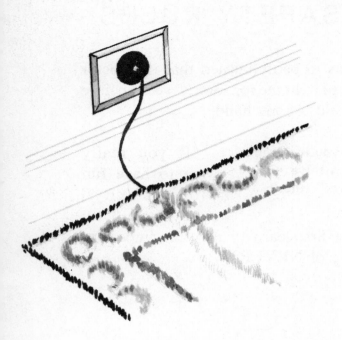

NEVER put electrical wires under carpets and rugs.

NEVER put a penny in the fuse box. Use the proper-sized fuse.

NEVER pull the chain of a light bulb if you are standing on a wet floor.

NEVER poke around the radio or television set if the switch is on.

NEVER touch an electrical appliance, switch, radio, or television set while bathing or when wet.

NEVER remain under or near a tree during an electrical storm or thunderstorm. Lightning may strike it.

NEVER remain in a lake during a thunderstorm.

NEVER, but never, touch a broken cable after or during a storm, or at any time. Call a policeman or fireman.

NEVER place anything except a plug into a wall socket.

"Remember," continued Dad as we listened very carefully, "electricity can be your friend or your enemy. You cannot argue with it. It will not forgive your mistakes. It will not accept your apology. It will reward you or punish you. It does not play favorites. Treat it with respect and understanding and it will serve you loyally."

DRY CELLS ARE THE SAFE WAY

DAD walked over to us and placed his hands on our shoulders. "Well, if you follow these NEVER rules, you will be doing the right thing. You can still have lots of fun with electricity if you work with dry cells. They cost little and you can carry them with you. You can put them in a box and take them to school, to the playground, to your friend's home or porch, and perform experiments. You can have a grand time. They are useful and safe."

Why should we never place a piece of metal across the two terminals? "Are there any NEVER rules for dry cells?" I asked. "Only one," said Dad. "NEVER put a piece of metal across the terminals. If you do, you will cause a short circuit and burn out the dry cell. Take care of these little power stations."

Dad opened my flashlight and removed the small dry cells. He gave one to my sister and one to me.

In how many ways can we use dry cells? "This fine invention is very useful to many people. What a help it is for those who have to walk in places where lighting a match or candle would be dangerous!

"When the farmer has to attend to his livestock in the barn, a match or candle could be very dangerous."

"That's right," said Susan Jane. "One slip and the whole barn could be set on fire."

"What about the coal miner who has to go poking around in the dark?" I suggested. "There are gases there that could cause an explosion if he lit a match."

"You are both right," said Dad. "And don't forget how Doctor Ross uses his flashlight to look at your throats. He carries it in his pocket like a fountain pen. The dry cell is used now more than ever before."

"How does a dry cell work?" I asked.

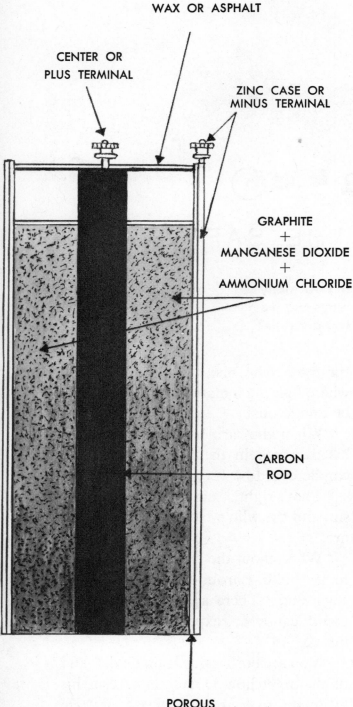

WAX OR ASPHALT

CENTER OR
PLUS TERMINAL

ZINC CASE OR
MINUS TERMINAL

GRAPHITE
+
MANGANESE DIOXIDE
+
AMMONIUM CHLORIDE

CARBON
ROD

POROUS
CARDBOARD

DIAGRAM OF A DRY CELL

"If you were to look inside one, you would see chemicals. They are ready to work — quietly and efficiently — to serve you when you press a button or flip a switch. There are no secret words to say to make it work. Anyone can learn how to do it. It's easy and it's fun. In fact, you can teach it to your friends.

Can you name some of the parts of a dry cell?

"Just as a magnet has two poles, north and south, so a dry cell has two poles, plus and minus. Do you see the center rod? That's made of carbon — the plus side. The case around the cell is usually made of a metal called zinc. That is the minus pole."

Why is it called a dry cell?

Dad took his hacksaw and cut a dry cell down the center.

"Now we are coming to the chemical plant that manufactures the electrical energy we sometimes call electrons. It's made into a hard paste so that it can be carried about. That's one of the reasons these cells are called 'dry cells.' "

Why is a storage battery called a "battery" and not a "cell"?

"Does our car use the same kind of battery or dry cell?" I asked.

"It is a battery, but not a dry cell," answered Dad. "The car battery is called a storage battery. It does not use a hard paste like your flashlight cell. We may call it a wet battery."

"A wet battery?" Susan Jane echoed.

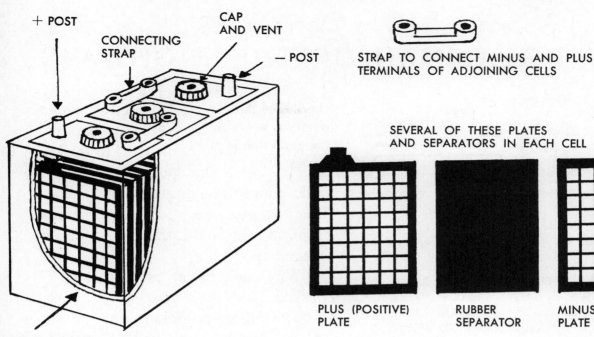

+ POST

CONNECTING STRAP

CAP AND VENT

— POST

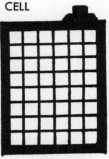

STRAP TO CONNECT MINUS AND PLUS TERMINALS OF ADJOINING CELLS

SEVERAL OF THESE PLATES AND SEPARATORS IN EACH CELL

PLUS (POSITIVE) PLATE

RUBBER SEPARATOR

MINUS (NEGATIVE) PLATE

CASE DIVIDED INTO 3 COMPARTMENTS OR CELLS

DIAGRAM OF A STORAGE BATTERY

What are the two liquids used in a storage battery?

"Right. It uses distilled water and an acid — a very dangerous acid."

"Do you mean that our car battery also makes electrons like a chemical plant?" I asked.

"A chemical plant is correct," smiled Dad. "The storage battery in our car is a real power station. It starts our motor and helps it run. It makes our light go on. It wipes the windows in a rainstorm. It runs our heater in the winter. It gives our radio power. My cigarette lighter uses the battery. Even the windows open and close in my new car, thanks to the battery."

"Why do we use distilled water? Is it cleaner?" I wanted to know.

"Why do we need acid, if it's so dangerous?" asked Susan Jane.

Why does the storage battery use distilled water?

"Distilled water, like rain water, does not have any impurities," said Dad. "And the acid combines with the lead to give us electricity. The car uses the battery to spark the gasoline in the motor to get it started. Without it the car wouldn't move."

Dad motioned for us to come over to his car. He raised the hood and we peered in to see the battery. "The storage battery in the car is not as safe to touch as the dry cell in your flashlight, Mike. The acid can cause a severe burn and make holes in our clothing.

"Do you remember the NEVER game?" Dad asked us.

"We sure do," answered my sister.

"Good. NEVER touch any part of the battery when the motor is on."

Mother walked over to us. "How would you junior scientists like to climb into this chemical or electrical or gasoline-operated machine and take a ride with me? I'll need some help with the groceries," she said.

THE POLICEMAN OF THE HIGHWAYS

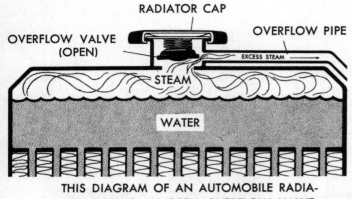

RADIATOR CAP

OVERFLOW VALVE (OPEN)

OVERFLOW PIPE

EXCESS STEAM

STEAM

WATER

THIS DIAGRAM OF AN AUTOMOBILE RADIATOR SHOWS AN OPEN OVERFLOW VALVE, ALLOWING EXCESS STEAM TO ESCAPE. SUCH A VALVE IS NEEDED IN ORDER TO RELIEVE STEAM PRESSURE.

How does the overflow valve in the automobile protect it?

THERE were many cars on the road to the supermarket, and a policeman was on duty directing traffic. Every so often he would stop the cars from moving until the traffic ahead cleared up.

"Why can't he let us go through?" I asked.

"The officer is looking out for our safety," Mother explained.

"He is like a safety valve," said Dad, "just as we have safety valves in locomotives and in the radiator of this car. These valves are seldom used, but they are very important. They are the policemen of these machines. When the locomotive has worked up too much steam and is in danger of exploding, the safety valve releases the extra steam. The same thing happens in the radiator of the car."

The policeman signaled us to go ahead.

ONE WAY

Why is the fuse often called the twenty-four-hour policeman?

"Just as the policeman stops traffic to make sure that the cars don't crash into one another, so a fuse in our home stops electrons from overcrowding. For when too many lines are plugged into one outlet, the electrons, like the cars, begin crashing into each other. When that happens, the extra movement makes the wires warm. The wires may get so hot that the walls of the house could catch fire.

"The fuse stops these electrons just as they begin to get hot. 'Stop,' says the policeman. 'Blow,' says the fuse. The lights go out. The toaster stops toasting and the broiler stops broiling."

"Too many electrical appliances were on at one time. They overloaded the circuit. That was one of the NEVER rules," I said.

"Very good, Mike. You learned quickly. It was a good thing that the fuse was there. Remember that the little fuse box is our policeman. It is guarding our home and our lives," said Dad. "Sometimes, instead of fuses, our houses have circuit breakers. These are safety devices, just like fuses. When too much current flows through the wires, the circuit breaker opens, which causes the electricity to stop flowing. Unlike fuses, circuit breakers can be reused."

A FUSE IS AN ELECTRICAL SAFETY DEVICE. WHEN TOO MUCH ELECTRIC CURRENT IS FLOWING, A PIECE OF METAL IN THE FUSE MELTS. THIS BREAKS THE CIRCUIT. WITHOUT A FUSE TO BREAK THE CIRCUIT, VERY STRONG CURRENT COULD CAUSE A FIRE.

ACTIVITIES FOR JUNIOR ELECTRICIANS

TRY these activities. Don't worry if you are not too successful at first. Follow the directions and diagrams as carefully as you can. You will have a great deal of fun.

Remember: When you see the word "wire" it means insulated wire. When it says, "connect wire," it means that the ends of the wire are to be stripped of insulation, material or paint.

NO. 1. HOW DOES YOUR FLASHLIGHT WORK?

You will use:
Flashlight
Piece of wire

Do this:

Turn your flashlight on and then off. Now that you are sure the flashlight works, take it apart to see the different parts.

Strip the insulation from both ends of a piece of wire about six inches long.

Wrap one end of the bare wire around the base of the bulb that you removed from the flashlight.

Touch the bottom of the bulb to the center terminal of the cell.

Touch the end of the wire to the bottom of the cell.

The light goes on.

Why it works:

When you closed the switch of the flashlight, you completed a circuit. That is, you provided a closed path for the current to follow in a circle.

LIGHT BULB

LENS

REFLECTOR

SWITCH

DRY CELLS

ZINC CONTAINER

METAL CASING

SPRING TO HOLD BATTERIES TOGETHER AND MAKE CONTACT

You will use:
- Dry cell (large or small)
- Flashlight bulb
- Miniature socket
- Wire
- Piece of metal
- Block of wood
- Two nails
- Hammer

Do this:

Do you remember *Activity No. 1?* We were able to turn the light on by touching the wire to the cell.

Then we removed the wire and the light went out.

That's pretty simple. But an easier way is to use a switch.

Take a piece of metal — four inches long, and one inch wide. (You can cut it from a tin can if you are careful.)

Nail one end of it on the block of wood.

Place another nail in the wood under the other end of the metal.

Do not place either nail all the way down in the wood.

Be sure that the loose end of the metal is not resting on the nail beneath.

Now you have a switch.

Connect one wire from either terminal of the dry cell to the nail under the metal.

Remember to strip off the insulation from the ends of all the wires you use.

Connect a second wire from the other terminal of the dry cell to either terminal of the miniature socket.

Connect a third wire from the other terminal of the socket to the nail holding the strip of metal in place.

Now press the switch.

If you have made all the connections properly, the circuit is closed and the light will go on.

Save this switch. You will use it many times in these activities.

Why it works:

If you have a large dry cell, you will notice two terminals at the top. Connecting wires to them is done much more easily than with the small flashlight cell.

But all of these activities can be done with either cell, except that the large cell lasts longer and it is easier to use.

Each cell gives us 1½ volts.

Connect the wires the way you did in *Activity No. 1.*

The switch is a convenient way for us to open and close a circuit. It is easier than connecting and disconnecting wires. It is also a safer way to turn the lights and other electrical appliances on and off.

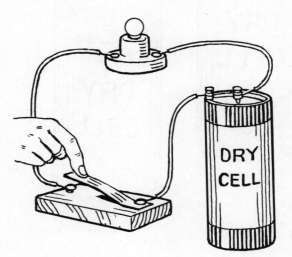

NO. 3. HOW CAN WE CONNECT TWO DRY CELLS TO GIVE US MORE POWER THAN ONE CELL?

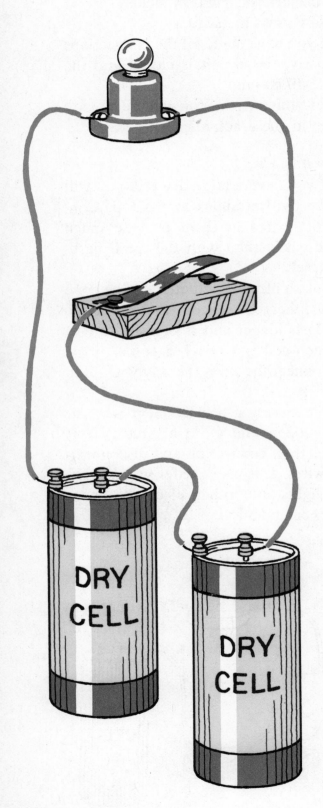

You will use:
    Two dry cells
    Wire
    Switch
    Flashlight bulb
    Miniature socket

Do this:

Do you remember how bright the bulb was in *Activity No. 2?* Now let's see what happens when we add another dry cell to the circuit. Of course, it has to be connected properly.

Connect one wire between the center terminal of cell 1 and the end terminal of cell 2.

The remainder of the connections are similar to the way you did them in the previous activity.

One wire is connected between the terminal of cell 1 and a socket terminal, and a second wire connects the other socket terminal to either nail on the switch.

The last wire connects the other nail with cell 2's center terminal.

Press the switch.

See how much brighter the light bulb is?

Why it works:

The two dry cells connected in series resulted in about twice the power of one cell.

This made the bulb brighter.

When you connected two cells of 1½ volts each in series, you really added them.

How many volts do you have now?

Would you like to try it with an electric bell?

NO. 4. HOW CAN WE CONNECT TWO DRY CELLS TO MAKE THEM LAST LONGER?

You will use:
  Two dry cells
  Wire
  Switch
  Flashlight bulb
  Miniature socket

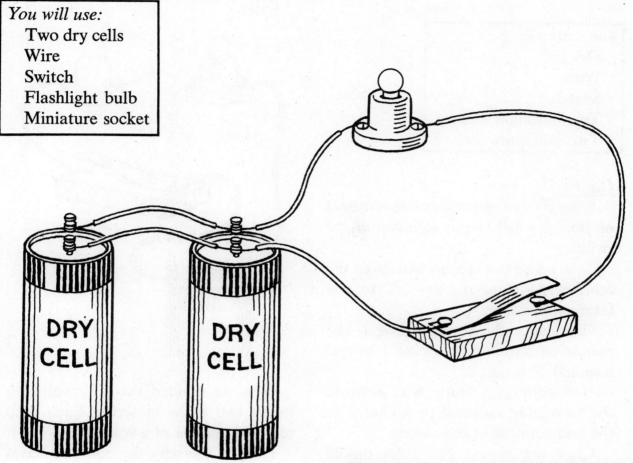

Do this:

Connect the dry cells, wires, switch and bulb as shown in the illustration.

First connect one dry cell in a circuit with your switch and the light bulb.

If you have forgotten how to do it, go back to *Activity No. 2.*

Now connect two other wires to the terminals on cell 2.

Take the wire from the center terminal of cell 2 and connect it to the center terminal of cell 1.

Take the wire coming from the end terminal of cell 2 and connect it to the end terminal of cell 1.

You should now have two wires connected to each of the terminals of cell 1.

Press the switch.

Notice that the light is not any brighter than it was when only one cell was in the circuit.

Why it works:

You connected the two dry cells in parallel.

No, the light is not brighter than it was with one dry cell.

That is why parallel connections are better when cells are to be used over a long period of time.

NO. 5. HOW CAN WE CONNECT SEVERAL LIGHT BULBS IN SERIES?

You will use:
    Dry cell
    Wire
    Switch
    Two flashlight bulbs
    Two miniature sockets

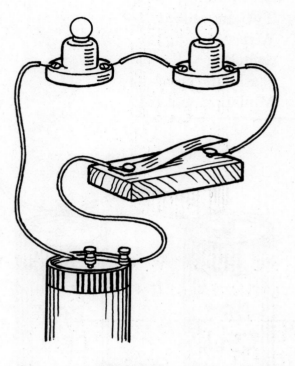

Do this:

Connect one wire from one terminal of your dry cell to one terminal of the switch.

Now connect a second wire from the other terminal of the dry cell to one terminal of socket 1.

Connect a third wire between the remaining terminal of socket 1 to one terminal of socket 2.

Now connect a fourth wire between the remaining terminal of socket 2 to the last terminal of the switch.

Close the switch. The bulbs should light.

Each bulb is not as bright as it was when we used one in our circuit.

Now unscrew one bulb. The other bulb will go out.

Why it works:

When both bulbs were lit, electricity was flowing in a complete path through the circuit. It was able to flow out of the dry cell right through the bulbs and return to the dry cell — like a merry-go-round.

This is called connecting bulbs in series.

In *Activity No. 2* we used one dry cell having 1½ volts to light one bulb. The little bulb was bright.

Now we divided that 1½ volts between two bulbs in series. Each bulb received only ¾ of a volt.

Do you see why the bulbs in series were a bit dim?

When you unscrewed one bulb, the other one went out.

Do you know why?

Because you interrupted the circuit. The electrons were not flowing in a merry-go-round.

Oh, yes, did you know that the tiny wire in the little bulb you removed was part of the path through which the electrons flow?

Our homes, stores and offices are all wired in parallel. If they were connected in series, all of the lights would be on and appliances running at one time or not at all. Wiring in parallel is surely more practical!

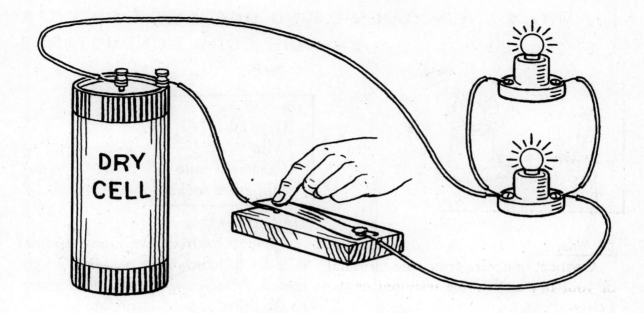

DRY CELL

NO. 6. HOW CAN WE CONNECT SEVERAL LIGHT BULBS IN PARALLEL?

You will use:
Dry cell
Wire
Switch
Two flashlight bulbs
Two miniature sockets

Do this:

Connect your dry cell, switch and one socket in a complete circuit.

Press the switch. See how bright it is? Try to remember how it looks.

Now we are going to bring another bulb into our circuit.

In *Activity No. 5* we connected them in series.

Do you remember the disadvantages of that circuit?

Connect a wire between one terminal of socket 1, already in the circuit, to one terminal of socket 2.

Now connect another wire between the other terminals of sockets 1 and 2. Notice that there are two wires com-ing out of each terminal of socket 1.

Press the switch. Both bulbs should light.

Are you surprised to find that each bulb is just as bright as the single bulb you lit at the start of this activity?

Now unscrew one bulb. The other one remains lit.

More surprises!

Why it works:

You have connected two bulbs in parallel.

Each bulb has its own path to and from the dry cell.

The path does not have to go through both bulbs as it did in a series circuit.

Try tracing the path of the electric current to each bulb.

Since each bulb is connected directly to the dry cell, each is as bright as if you had only one bulb.

Now if one bulb goes out, the other remains lit, as in your own house.

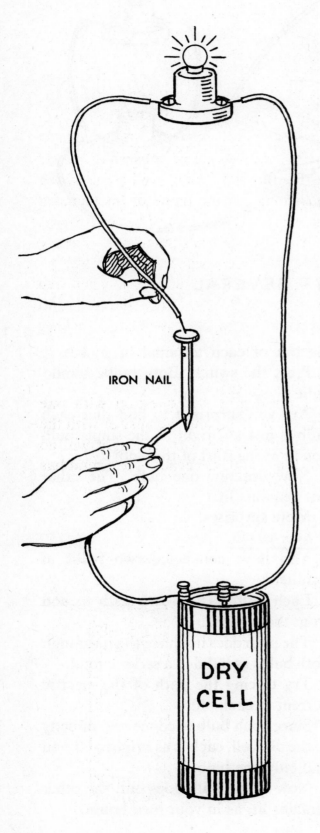

IRON NAIL

DRY CELL

You will use:
Dry cell
Wire
Flashlight bulb
Miniature socket

Do this:

Connect a wire between one terminal of a dry cell and one terminal of a light socket. Attach one end of another wire to the other dry cell terminal.

Attach a third wire to the other terminal of the socket.

The ends of the two wires should be free.

Touch the two free ends of the wire together briefly.

You have now completed the circuit and the light should go on.

Touch the two free ends of the wires to opposite ends of an iron nail. The light will go on.

Test other materials in this manner to see which ones help the light go on.

Why it works:

Until now we have used wires to complete our circuits. We saw how a nail acted in the same way.

As you see, some metals are good conductors of electricity. Some are better than others.

If you test glass, wood, plastic, or rubber, you will find that the light will not go on. Not enough electricity passes through them to light the bulb.

These materials are called non-conductors.

You will use:
  Dry cell
  Wire
  Flashlight bulb
  Miniature socket
  Cardboard
  Nail

Do this:

Use the nail to punch six holes down the left side of a piece of cardboard, and six holes down the right side.

Place the end of one wire in any hole at the left and the other end in any hole at the right.

Strip the insulation from the ends of the wire and secure it in place.

Repeat this with five other wires.

You now have six wires in place in a haphazard way.

Set this aside for a while.

Connect a wire between a dry cell terminal and a socket terminal.

Connect another wire to the remaining terminal of the dry cell.

Now attach a third wire to the remaining terminal of the socket.

This is similar to your conductor tester in *Activity No. 7.*

Touch the two free ends of the wires together briefly. The light will go on.

Hold the cardboard so that you cannot see how the wires are connected.

Place the name of a baseball player on the left side, which will serve as the question, and the name of his team on the right side, which will be the answer.

Be sure that the player and team are on opposite ends of the same wire.

Ask your friend to take the two free ends of the wires from the cell and socket. Now try to touch the matching questions and answers.

Why it works:

By touching the question with one end of the wire, and the answer with the other end of the wire, the light will go on. This happens because the circuit has been completed.

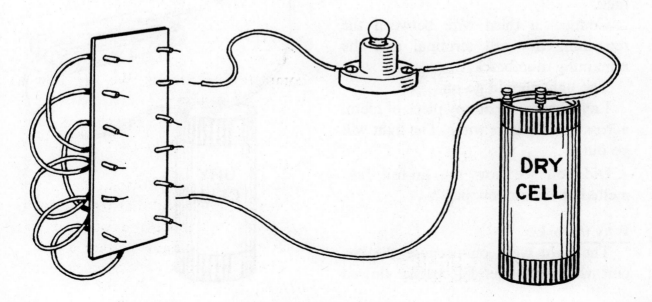

You will use:
Dry cell
Wire
Flashlight bulb
Miniature socket
Tin foil
Block of wood
Two thumbtacks

Do this:

Cut a piece of tin foil so that the center is as thin as a piece of wire.

Secure it to a block of wood with two thumbtacks. Do not push the tacks all the way down. Set this aside for a while.

Strip about two inches of insulation away from the middle portion of two wires. Connect these wires to the two terminals of a miniature socket.

Connect the other end of one of these wires to a dry cell terminal.

Connect the other end of the second wire to one of the thumbtacks of your fuse board.

Be sure that the stripped end of the wire is in contact with the metal of the tack.

Connect a third wire between the remaining dry cell terminal and the remaining thumbtack.

The light should go on.

Lay a bare wire or any piece of metal across the two bare wires. The light will go out.

Did you see how the tin-foil fuse melted at the narrow part?

Why it works:

The light went on because the circuit was complete. Electricity flowed through the tin-foil fuse, as it does in our homes.

When you placed a piece of metal across the two bared wires, you caused a short circuit. Electricity was able to flow back to the dry cell without passing through the bulb to light it.

The electricity that was not used by the bulb caused the wires to become hotter. The tin-foil strip melts at a lower temperature than the other wires. When this happened, the circuit was broken and no more electricity flowed.

The fuse protects us by burning out. If the fuse were not there, the wires would have become hotter and hotter. This could have resulted in a fire.

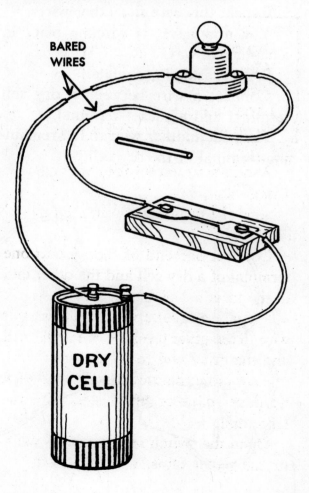

BARED WIRES

DRY CELL

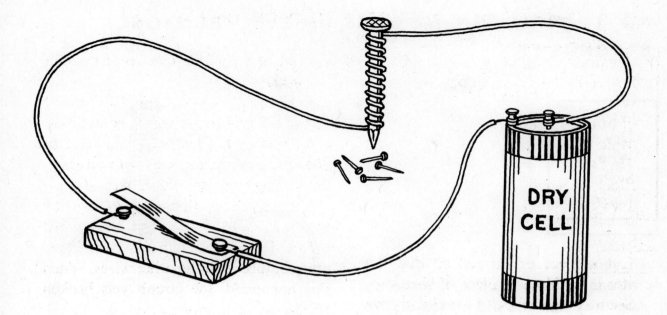

NO. 10. HOW CAN WE MAKE AN ELECTROMAGNET?

You will use:
Dry cell
Wire
Switch
Large nail
Small nails or paper clips

Do this:

Wind about ten turns of wire around a large nail.

Strip the insulation from the ends of the wire.

Connect one end of the wire to one terminal of a dry cell and the other end to the terminal of the switch.

Prepare a second wire. Connect this wire to the other terminal of the dry cell and the other end to the switch.

Now close the switch and try to pick up paper clips or small nails with the large nail.

Open the switch and the small nails, or the paper clips, will fall down.

Why it works:

The electricity from one part of the dry cell flows through the many turns of wire back into the dry cell.

When electricity flows through a wire, the wire has magnetic power around it. If the wire happens to be in the form of a coil, the magnetism is even stronger.

Now, when we put an iron nail inside the coil, the nail becomes a magnet. This is true only for as long as the electricity is flowing in the circuit. It is a magnet when you want it to be.

Do you see how magnets and electricity are related?

Our magnet really depends on the electricity it gets from the dry cell.

We find electromagnets all around us.

We find them in refrigerators, in television sets, telephones, in Dad's electric shaver and in Mother's vacuum cleaner.

NO. 11. HOW CAN WE MAKE AN ELECTROMAGNET STRONGER?

You will use:
Dry cell
Wire
Switch
Large nail
Small nails

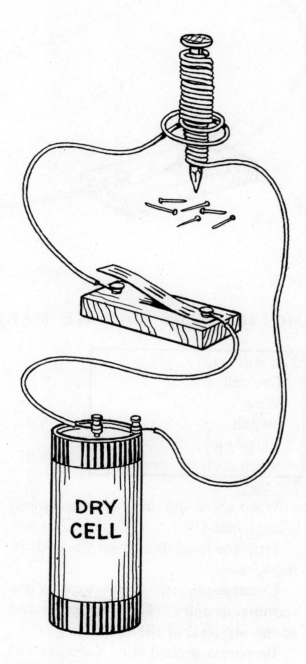

Do this:

Connect your electromagnet in the same way that you did in *Activity No. 10* — except for one thing. This time wind *twenty-five* turns of wire around the large nail.

Close the switch. See how many small nails you can pick up.

Do this two more times.

Do you know how to find the average number of nails picked up?

Add the number of nails picked up in three tries. Then divide by three.

This will give you the average number of nails picked up by the electromagnet with the twenty-five turns of wire.

Write the average down.

Now that you are an expert, wrap twenty-five more turns of wire around the nail, making fifty turns all together.

Count the number of nails you can pick up this time. Do this two more times.

Find the average number of nails picked up by your electromagnet with fifty turns of wire. Write this down.

Compare the two averages. You will see that more nails were picked up by the electromagnet with more turns.

Why it works:

The more turns of wire you have, the more magnetism there is around the coil, and the stronger the electromagnet.

You may have found that you picked up about twice as many nails when you doubled the number of turns.

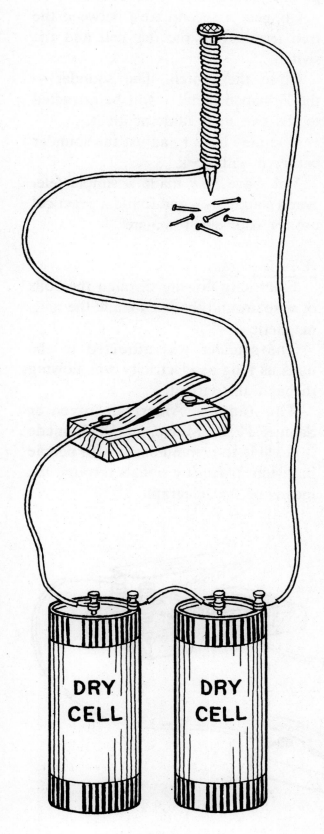

You will use:
Two dry cells
Wire
Switch
Large nail
Small nails

Do this:

Do you remember how to connect two dry cells in series to give us more electricity?

You must remember to connect one wire between the plus or center terminal of one dry cell to the minus or end terminal of the other cell.

Connect a second wire from the other terminal of one cell to one terminal of the switch.

Wrap twenty-five turns of wire around a large nail.

Connect one end of the electromagnet to the free terminal of the cell and the other end to the switch.

Close the switch and see how many nails you can pick up. Try it three times to find an average number.

How does it compare with the number picked up previously?

Why it works:

When we connect two dry cells in series, we get twice as much electricity than we do with one cell. That is, we get 3 instead of 1½ volts from one cell.

Then we can be sure that if we want a stronger magnet, we must send more electricity through the coils.

You will use:
Dry cell
Wire
Switch
Two nails
Screw
Piece of metal
Block of wood

Do this:

Bend the piece of metal into the Z-shape shown in the diagram.

Nail it on the block of wood.

Hammer two nails into the wood so that they are just under the free end of the metal strip.

Connect a fairly long length of wire to one terminal of a dry cell.

Wind the wire several times around one of the nails, beginning at the top and working down.

Then bring the wire across to the other nail and wind it around as many times as the other one, working upward.

Connect the other end of this wire to one terminal of your switch.

Connect a second wire between the free terminal of the dry cell and the switch.

Close the switch. The sounder — the Z-shaped metal — will be attracted to the two nails underneath it.

You may have to adjust the sounder before it will work.

You have now made a simple telegraph sounder — and found a practical use for your electromagnet.

Why it works:

Electricity flowing through the coils of wire around the nails made the nails magnetic.

The sounder was attracted to the nails as long as electricity was flowing through the circuit.

The famous American inventor Samuel F. B. Morse, in 1844, made it possible to communicate with people in distant places by signals through the means of the telegraph.

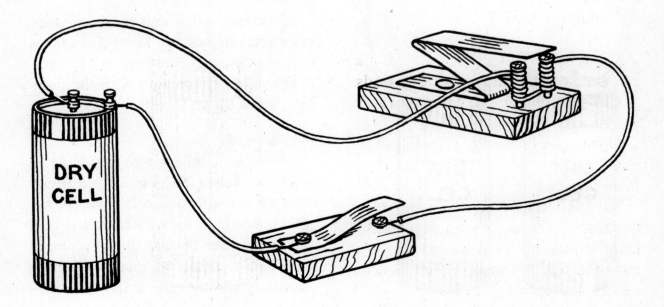

NO. 14. HOW CAN WE MAKE AN ELECTRIC CURRENT DETECTOR?

You will use:
  Dry cell
  Long wire
  Magnetic compass
  Block of wood
  Cover of small cardboard box
  Four thumbtacks
  Two paper clips

Do this:

Wrap about ten turns of insulated wire around the cover of a box.

Strip the insulation from the ends of the wire.

Place the box on a block of wood and secure it in place with some thumbtacks.

Bend two paper clips in half, as shown.

Wrap the ends of the wires around the thumbtacks. Slip the paper clips under the tacks before pressing them into the wood.

The paper clips will be your leads.

Place your magnetic compass inside the box.

Connect a wire between a dry cell terminal and a switch terminal.

Connect two other wires from the cell and switch to the paper clip leads.

Close the switch. The compass needle will move.

Open and close the switch several times.

Why it works:

Do you remember that when electricity moves through a coil, magnetism is all around it? That magnetism goes right through the glass to the magnetic needle and moves it.

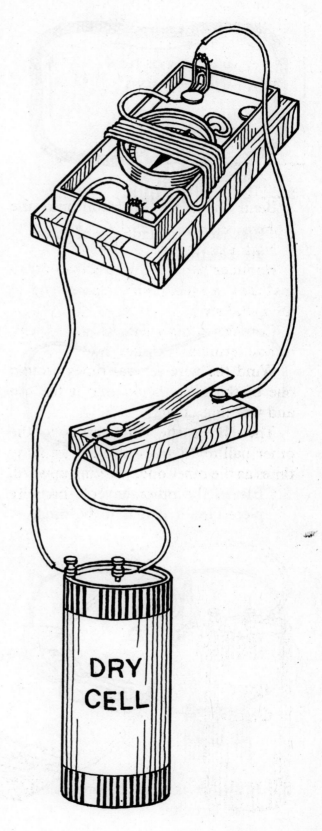

Some of the important ideas presented in this book are summarized below. As you read them, you may want to go back and refresh your memory.

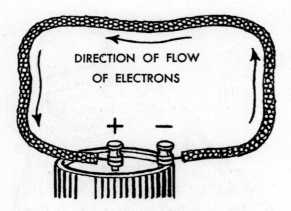

1. Electricity is made up of moving electrons.

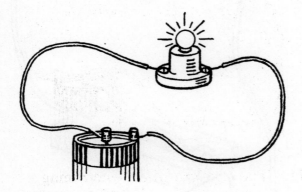

2. Electricity must have a complete circuit if it is to be used.

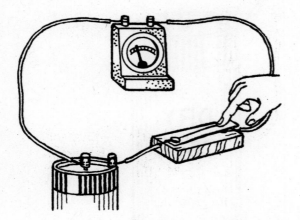

3. A switch is used to open and close circuits.

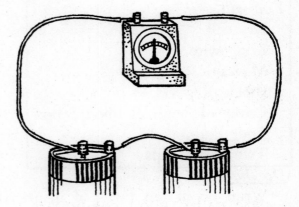

4. More than one cell connected in series will give more power than a single cell.

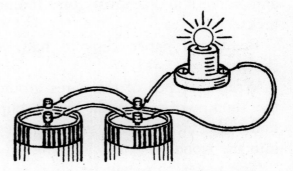

5. More than one cell connected in parallel will give longer life than a single cell.

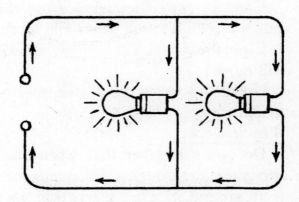

6. Lights in our homes are wired in parallel.

7. Some materials, particularly metals, carry electricity better than others. These materials are called good conductors.

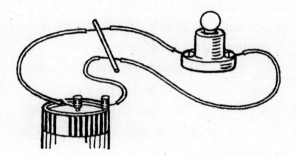

8. A short circuit occurs when the current can flow through an easy short cut instead of going through the regular circuit.

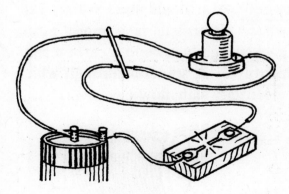

9. A fuse protects us from damage due to short circuits, or from using too much electricity at the same time.

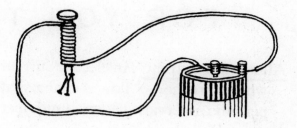

10. Electricity flowing through a coil of wire around an iron core, makes the core into a magnet for as long as electricity is flowing. This is an electromagnet.

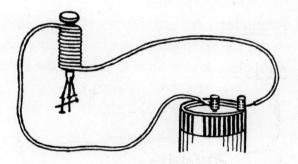

11. The strength of an electromagnet can be increased by increasing the number of coil turns.

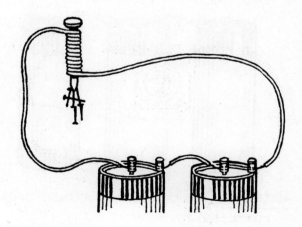

12. The strength of an electromagnet can also be increased by adding dry cells to the circuit.

SOME IMPORTANT TERMS
FOR YOU TO REMEMBER

Alternating current: An electric current whose direction of flow is changed at periodic intervals (many times per second).

Ammeter: An instrument for measuring the strength of an electric current.

Ampere: A unit that measures the rate of flow of electric current.

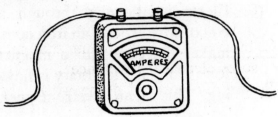

Atom: The tiniest part of an element.

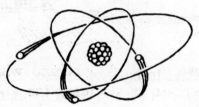

Battery: Two or more electrical cells connected together.

Circuit: Entire path along which electricity can flow from the source through wires and appliances and back to the source.

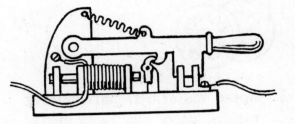

Circuit breaker: An automatic switch which breaks the circuit when too much electricity is flowing. It is similar to a fuse, but it can be reused.

Compound: A substance formed by a combination of elements.

Conductor: A good carrier of electricity. It acts as a highway.

Direct current: An electric current that flows in only one direction through a circuit.

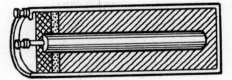

Dry cell: A self-contained voltaic cell whose electrolyte is a moist paste packed tightly around a carbon rod.

Electrolyte: A solution through which electricity can flow.

Electromagnet: A coil of wire wound around an iron core which becomes a magnet as long as electricity flows through the coil.

Electron: A negative or minus charge of electricity, the smallest now known.

Element: A substance made up of only one kind of atom.

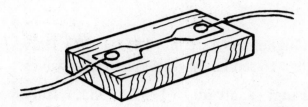

Fuse: A device which acts as a policeman to warn us of danger. The fuse melts when too many electrons are flowing. This breaks the circuit.

Galvanometer: An instrument for detecting direct currents of electricity.

Generator: A machine or dynamo that produces electricity from mechanical energy.

Horsepower: A unit for measuring power.

Insulator: A very poor conductor of electricity.

Kilowatt: One thousand watts.

Molecule: The tiniest part of a compound.

Ohm: A unit of measurement to gauge the resistance to the passage of electric current.

Ohmmeter: An instrument that measures electrical resistance.

Power: The rate of doing work.

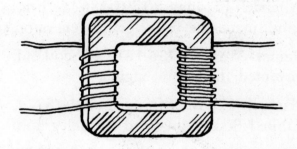

Transformer: A machine which can increase or decrease the voltage of an alternating current.

Volt: A unit that measures electrical pressure.

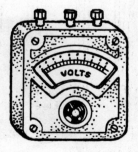

Voltmeter: A device for measuring voltage.

Watt: A unit for measuring electrical power.

SOME FAMOUS SCIENTISTS WHO MADE THE ELECTRICAL AGE POSSIBLE

Alessandro Volta (1745-1827), Italy, made the first cell that produced an electric current.

André Marie Ampère (1775-1836), France, developed the science of electromagnetism.

Georg Simon Ohm (1787-1854), Germany, worked with current electricity.

Michael Faraday (1791-1867), England, made the first electric generator.

James Watt (1736-1819), Scotland, invented the steam engine.

Samuel F. B. Morse (1791-1872), United States, invented the telegraph.

Alexander Graham Bell (1847-1922), United States, invented the telephone.

Guglielmo Marconi (1874-1937), Italy, first to send a message over radio waves.

Luigi Galvani (1737-1798), Italy, discovered that electricity is possible by chemical action.

Thomas Alva Edison (1847-1931), United States, invented the electric light bulb.

Hans Christian Oersted (1777-1851), Denmark, found that electricity and magnetism are related.

Charles Proteus Steinmetz (1865-1923), United States, made many contributions in the field of electrical engineering.

VOLTA

FARADAY

AMPERE

BELL